Agnes Caldwell

Reflective Moments Dawning

By
Agnes Caldwell

Bloomington, IN   Milton Keynes, UK

authorHOUSE™

AuthorHouse™
1663 Liberty Drive, Suite 200
Bloomington, IN 47403
www.authorhouse.com
Phone: 1-800-839-8640

AuthorHouse™ UK Ltd.
500 Avebury Boulevard
Central Milton Keynes, MK9 2BE
www.authorhouse.co.uk
Phone: 08001974150

First published by AuthorHouse 3/28/2006

ISBN: 1-4259-1692-9 (sc)
ISBN: 1-4259-1691-0 (dj)

Printed in the United States of America
Bloomington, Indiana

This book is printed on acid-free paper.

Acknowledgements

I would like to mention those who helped in many ways, to make this little book possible.

My friends and family who encouraged me to keep writing.
My daughters Judy, Kathy, Debby, and Karen, who type much better than I.
My son Larry, who also typed much of the originals. His Kentucky River trip picture appears in this book.
His sudden death in 2004 has left a void where only memories and faith sustain me.
To my numerous friends who often requested a special poem written for a special event or person in their lives, reflected on many of these pages.

My sincere appreciation to each of you.

Dedication

I dedicate this book to my only son Larry, who died suddenly of a massive heart attack on August 2nd, 2004, the day after his forty-seventh birthday.
He was always encouraging me to get on with getting this book put together. Just days before his death he offered to do all the typing I needed. I had no idea he was so ill, or that he would soon be gone from us.

I know where he is today, he can see that I finally did it, and I'm sure he's happy and smiling.

Table of Contents

Thoughts and Feelings...

Devotions...

Prayers and Encouragement....

Writer's Thoughts.....

Introspection

I stand alone, I am not made of glass
No one can see my thoughts
I must tell them to someone,
or write them for someone to read
If I speak and no one listens, I feel bad,
rejected, unloved, devalued.
If I write something, perhaps
Someone may read it someday and feel less
lonely.

Without sound, I have spoken.
Without being there, I have touched.
Only a reader knows that touch.
From a passive piece of paper,
Words can leap for joy,
or weep in sorrow.
Only a writer knows that feeling.
That special creative release of energy.

Special Greeting

Today I stopped at a card shop
Pretty verses, I read quite a few
Of all the cards they had written
Not one was especially for you

So I bought a pen and some paper
A gold pen and the paper is blue
Golden glow of the sun and blue sky
Conveys the way I feel about you

Sunlight and roses forever
That's what I'm wishing for you
A life filled with gladness and laughter
May your heavens forever stay blue

Life's and Nature's Changing Seasons.......

Wooded Green

Walking in a mountain woodland,
The dark hush surrounds me
Spongy dead leaves cushion each step,
And moss covers tree trunks, long fallen.

I hear the rustle of moving leaves as
Small animals hurry about the business of
living.
Maybe they heard me and didn't know,
I only want to share this quiet retreat
From the blazing July sun.

This cool green oasis so far removed from
The rush of modern living.
Unchanged for centuries, a peaceful haven
to which I will return.
My hidden paradise.

Flames

Passionate flames that leap
Like a forest fire devouring it's victim
Caught in it's own intensity,
Unbridled heat of the moment,
Propelled by the wind of it's own invention

Driven, scorching, searing,
Paying homage to no earthly power, or
Persuasion
It is bent on total destruction
Not unlike human flesh, it must have oxygen,
Without which it diminishes with
The swiftness of light
Glory so powerful, so suddenly
Nothing at all

God's Masterpiece

Oh tree that stands and reaches up
Toward skies either cloudy or fair
Oh tree with branches of lovely green
Or winters tree that is lonely and bare

Oh summers tree whose lovely shade
Is a place to stop and rest
Your arms outstretched in welcome
As birds return to build their nest

In wintertime a barren silhouette
Stands out against the blanket of white
Reminds one that life is ever changing
Even the tree waits through the night

Morning comes and it's spring again
Green things are once more growing
Oh tree, a constant reminder of
God's love forever flowing

The Mighty Pacific

Pulsating against hard rocks
breathing misty spray
upon remains of
stormy seas past

Restless, never tiring,
lulled only by the warmth
of gathering storms

She obeys no command,
No one has ever controlled her
Except one,
The Master of the universe

Larry loved natures wonders. Here, on his trip down The Kentucky River in 1998, he felt he experienced what he imagined his ancestors lived in the 1800's.

Kentucky River

Kentucky River winding,
Flowing around those green, green hills
Those memories stay with me
I know they always will
Tho' I may not see them
Sometimes for a long, long time.
Just to recall that mountain scene
Can rest my weary mind

Sometimes it's muddy water
When the heavy rains abound
Then it's that rich mountain soil
Just flowing 'round and 'round
Some of it will settle
Where farmers like to sow
The seeds will have all they need
Just watch how big they grow

Kentucky flowing gently
Into the Ohio
Then to the Mississippi
And the gulf below
Some people like the ocean
The cruise ships out at sea
In a row boat on that river
Is where I'd rather be

Kentucky Mountain River, keep flowing to the sea

Storms

The winter storm has passed, I heard the lonely
howling wind, as it passed my window.
It's icy fingers desperately tearing at any
crevice, trying to enter my humble dwelling.

Had I looked out, I would have seen, under the
streetlight, swinging to and fro, snow driven
by the merciless wind, in its mad rush to
heaven knows where.

By dawn the wind may be gone, and in the
early morning light, all will be pure white
stillness. The rounded soft contours of snow,
covering everything, will speak of calm, and
one can hardly imagine the storm that raged
at midnight.

Life is like that, it seems, youth with a mad
rush of desire, passions that drive one into
every facet of endeavor.

There are also moments of quiet stillness when
all is peaceful. Rare they may be, yet we
need these lulls to renew our strength, to
fortify our resistance against any storm life
may send us.

Until all is calm again, then we can say,
the storm has passed.

A Spider's Art

I walked this path just yesterday
And I know it wasn't there
That spider web of fine design
That shines like silken hair
What toil the spider must have spent
Through the dark of summers night
To weave the squares so perfectly
And make it turn out right

Now as a newly awakened sun
Creeps from her eastern bed
Light rays caress the spider's art
Gently turn it to golden thread
Enraptured I stare at the magic scene
Dripping wet fields of greenest corn
Draped in many hued morning glories
And spiders leave their "art" to the morn

Country Sights and Sounds

Misty, lazy, slowly waking
Sunlight creeps gently through
Brilliantly illuminating
Green leaves wet with dew
Midday passes swiftly
Evening shadows creep
Twilight's lullaby sounds,
Subdued, restful for sleep
Stars claim the heavens
Birds settle into their nests
Lights out, kitchen is dark now
Chores finished, time to rest

Tinkle, tinkle, a cowbell
Slight movement out in the barn
Far away the owls, "who whooo"
A night call meaning no harm
Meadows glowing with fireflies
An occasional bark of a dog
Crickets have their own choir for summer
From the swamp the croak of a frog

Necessary Change

Maple's dress lies on the ground,
　　she stands shamelessly naked.
Gracious and elegant she poses,
　　limbs reach out to the universe.
Is it surrender, or a gesture
　　to bless her gift of the season?
She looks vulnerable, however,
　　she will now rely on her roots.
They go deep and will surely sustain her
　　through the bitter cold of winter.

Setting Sail

May the sun sparkle off calm waters.
May you always set your sails toward new
adventures.
May the sunsets you view be golden
masterpieces.
Let each sunrise be a glorious beginning.
And each rainy day end with a beautiful
rainbow.

Rainy Saturday

The days grow gradually shorter, and the stillness is creeping over the land. Small creatures have found their winter hiding places, and birds have gone south in large flocks, which darkened the sky for many days. The rain began before daybreak and dismally continues.

Summer's enthusiasm and drive diminishes into a melancholy lazy disinterest. One wonders will this go on forever? Yet at the same time we feel in harmony with this vacuum between seasons. This one time of the year when we are slowed enough to allow our "true self", our soul, to catch up. To rest and reason on the why of our existence.

Storm Tossed

Will I forever be besieged with uncertainties?
Will I ever be blessed with the joy security
brings?
Will calm, peace, and contentment ever be my
companion?
Will life end in a flurry of confusion?

Or, will a turning of the tide bring this
capricious shallop into tranquil waters, and the
sunrise of tomorrow, in radiance, dissipate the
murky gloom?
May its luminous afterglow give warmth and
faith, where doubt once lurked.

The Returning

Let's take a long vacation
Just you and I alone
Not to some tropic island
But to our former home

A place where hills majestic
Stand guard the valley green
Where nature flaunts her wonders
The best I've ever seen

Gracious hills and greenest valleys
So restful to the soul
And if I'm feeling weary
That view can make me whole

The memories that I cherish
Come rushing over me
When I'm tired of other places
Kentucky is where I'll be

Agnes Caldwell

Summer Symphony

On a morning like this, negative thoughts
elude me. Worries of yesterday I can't recall.
Sunbeams dance in my garden, among
flowers, where bumblebees and butterflies
kiss the waiting fragile blossoms.

I wonder if the flowers have a song of
fulfillment and exaltation, inaudible to my ear,
yet in harmony with the whirling of wings.
As soft as footsteps of angels who step lightly
through my garden by night, whispering
secrets of tomorrow's colors, and leaving a
sparkle of dew on each tiny petal.

Sleeping Season

*Winter is not a death, but a sleeping.
White fields awaiting the changing of the
colors, guarded by the furred creatures
whose quest for survival allows them
not their leisure.*

*At the appointed time, all will awaken to
even more life at its beginning. Thus
given shade and shelter by the older
time tested, new tender young plants can
flourish in this wonderful continuum of
nature.*

Hello Spring!

Hello Robin,
I see you are early at the task of building.
Isn't it a fresh and wonderful world today,
washed by melted snow and recent rain,
swept by swift eastbound wind in search of
the ocean?
This morning only the light breeze touches
a kite caught in a tree, where leaves of
tomorrow peek at this bright world today.
of bikes, big wheels and roller skates begin
their spring fun campaign.
I, too, enjoy this quiet, yet vibrant hour as
spring unfolds once more.
Have a good day, little Robin.

Spring in the Hills

*Spring occurred with an effervescent burst of
vivid color.
Creatures small and swift of feet, dance to the
symphony of the many-voiced choir, whose
winged members flutter from tree to tree,
joyfully adding tones harmoniously.
Wild roses blush pink, while white dogwood
blossoms adorn the hills.
Meadows lay a bright yellow dandelion carpet
and beyond, the redbud is dressed in her
brightest color for this spring parade.
The atmosphere is so clear, as if the sun has
driven every cloud away, save a few fluffy
white ones whose only function is to
show off the blue depth of infinite splendor
and wonder.
The fragrance of new life touches ones
sensibility, transferring us out of the mundane
until we feel as if we are a part of this
magnificent creative production we call
"spring."*

Frolic in the Sun

*Happy snowflakes bathed in sunlight dance
in the chill wind of this December day.
The sun seems all the brighter because
soon it will vanish behind a curtain
of gray clouds.
The air is filled with expectancy of happy
shoppers.
This joyous burst of enthusiasm and
goodwill not only gives a farewell to the
year past, but also leads us into the bleak,
cold months ahead.
Like a skier having reached the summit, we
glide graciously through January,
February, and by March we are ready for
spring breezes on a lower plain, where brooks
ripple with yesterday's snow.
The world, a stage where the scene is forever
changing.*

Agnes Caldwell

Autumn

*A collage of colors that only nature can
create.
Brushed by the cool wind of autumn
After the crisp frosty night, the sun appears
and gently erases the frosty film,
Bringing colors to their freshest, most brilliant
tones!
What glory! Autumn!*

October

The sun is brilliant
The atmosphere is so clear
Space looks like a blue forever
Trees aflame in gold and red
The air is light, refreshing
I breathe deeply, hungrily
Wanting to be filled with
The wonder and beauty of it all

Frosty Autumn

A glow touches the fallen leaves
The treetrunk casts a shadow
north and westward, a straight line
Bare branches and twigs create a
lacelike network against a bright blue sky
In the shadowed places a film of
white frost clings until warm brightness
touches

In Wonderment

Look up and see the starry heavens
The myriad stars light up this lowly earth
Their continued presence gives a mighty
feeling there's more.
We cannot fathom its worth
Reach out, move beyond survival
There's joy beyond the daily struggles here
There's hope, peace, and happiness awaiting
With faith and love we'll find it somewhere

See The Beauty

I think the thing that kept me sane
through troubled times were memories of
good things of childhood days.
I remember the sight of morning glories, covered
with dew, as we hurried off to our work in the fields.
Their brilliant colors almost breathtaking in
their array of hues. They grew so freely
up and around the corn.
I can recall Mom singing a hymn as she rushed
about her chores. She had a good attitude
about life. She was always busy, yet
was able to instruct with words of knowledge
as she labored. One of her lines was,
"Work won't hurt you, but worry can kill you."
Another was, "Real beauty comes from within."
Maybe the reason I like those is because they make
good sense. Work relieves tension, while worried
inactivity increases it.
The later keeps the focus on the real values of
personality rather than pride based on the surface
appearance.
I guess I was very lucky to be able to see the
beauty all around me.
The beauty only nature provides.
Being poor as far as money, and the things it allows
wasn't so important to a child in those days.
I was attuned to my surroundings and their
harmony.
This I believe was a blessing.

Memories....

My Journey

I walked many miles along a rocky road.
Alongside, bushes and thorns grew in
abundance.
Sometimes in trying to find better footing
I touched them, they tore my flesh.
I, so intent on the maneuver involved,
almost missed a smoother path leading in
another direction.
Many years passed before I went back
to see if it was as bad as I remembered.
Then I discovered it had been worse,
and something more in that long ago
journey.
I had passed two alternate roads without
seeing them, before I left that path of
destruction.
It has been a long journey just to realize
How lost I was back then.

Survivor

A memory of the railroad,
The work crew of about thirty black men
Bent to their task.
Their caps on backward to protect their neck
From the merciless southern summer sun.
Their blackness shiny from sweat.
Toiling under duress of the big man
Pistols strapped around his hips.
A man who valued not their lives,
Indifferent to human suffering.

As the crew lifted a rail of steel
A low musical sound vibrated
Bodies swinging back and forth
In rhythm to the exact moment
They dropped the rail into place.

Then the clanging sound of hammer
As the spikes were driven down
The singing would continue while they worked,
The harmony of souls unified in spirit.
I believe beyond deep despair
The soul seeks fulfillment
The foreman with the guns had no dominion
Over the souls that found
Freedom in song.

The Farm

Cartwheels and skinning cats
Hide and seek, such fun as that
Oh, the joy of childhood on the farm

Neighbors visit for Sunday fun
They had a son, who would kiss and run
Passing time one Sunday on the farm

Making a ball out of old sock twine
We could play a game another time
Children's game of baseball on the farm

Andyover, someone catch the ball!
It's coming over, look out, don't fall!
The roof is high for a small one on the farm

Burlap bag, the race is beginning
We were all in it, I no chance of winning
But I always tried everything on the farm

Clang, clang, the spike and the shoe
To get a ringer, I bet you do!
A game of skill was horseshoes on the farm

Four decades later, looking back
Memories of walking that railroad track
To catch a train to leave childhood,
and the farm

Agnes Caldwell

Life is Like a River

To walk that mountain road again
To see that spring so cool and clear
To feel that youthful innocence
To leave the cares that found me here

It was summertime in Lee County
A child, I was awed by the scene
I'd never seen such dewey mornings
I'd never seen such shades of green

Way down below flows the river
On to some distant sea it goes
I knew one day I would follow
Where I would end I did not know

Take me back to Lee County
Just so my memories can recall
Days of youth and life's sweet promise
The prayer I had to live it all

On to life beyond the mountain
That other world I longed to see
Dreams of youth so often shattered
When sweet dreams become reality

Mountain Memories

As I neared the spring, the evening hush
had settled over the woodland.
I felt suddenly alone with the mountain.
The rocks supplied generously,
the cold clear water I had climbed
the rocky mountain for.
I filled the pails and swiftly made my return
down the mountain road.
Sunlight was fading.
It always struck me anew,
how suddenly darkness came in these hills.
The river flowed like a velvet ribbon below.
It too, could change suddenly
during a rainy season.

Back Home

Just a trip of country memories
Down the river deep and wide
The water ripples softly
Like my feelings deep inside

For many years I wandered
To far away distant shores
Now I contemplate these connections
With each stroke of the oar

Yes, a man can return
To where a child once roamed
His awareness, it's only a visit
Really shows how much he has grown

Days of Long Ago – Fast Forward

It has been many years ago, yet I remember
The fun we had as children out at play
Now time has changed, the neighborhood is
quieter, no happy laughter,
The children gone away

There are special places for their recreation
No basket hangs high over "Dad's" garage
door
Now, may I ask, what happened to freedom
Where we can't see children playing anymore?

The family home disappeared
Behind a barnlike condominium
Parking space for only those who live there.
No parking on any street,
Slow to 25 and keep on driving
No turn, one way
Is your seatbelt fastened?

Oh please, will someone tell me
Where did all our freedom go?

Momentary Flashback

This morning a squirrel crossed my path,
a walnut in his mouth
He is preparing for the winter months ahead
He transported me to days when we sawed
wood with a crosscut, then stored it in the
shed for the cold season.

Then memories of our family sitting
near the warmth of fire, and Mom reading,
or popping corn in a covered pan.
The little squirrel doesn't realize he made my
day brighter

Agnes Caldwell

Good Ole' Days

People talk of the good ole' days
Those days have come and gone
What we have are these new ways
Where you cannot buy a home

It's condo and apartment rent
You pay but never own
No one ever seems to care
So you must manage all alone

So find the latest Internet
They say it's got it all
Something to entertain you
Or give someone a call

Telephone bills are out of sight
Credit to the limit
Every time you touch that dial
They charge you by the minute

It's rocket blasts and satellites
Bombs that crash the planes
Security here, scanners there
I.D. cards to prove your name

So, now and then, if we go back
To days that used to be
It's memories way to save the day
For those longing to be free!

Reflection

Time is never wasted,
just doing nothing is all right.
It allows me to reflect on the many things,
happenings, and people in my past,
who have inspired me.
Many times when the "going on,"
would have been too scary an undertaking,
if not for certain persons' encouragement.
I will always be grateful for friends and family.
They were God's blessing,
my work was his assignment.
My journey is his triumph, because,
I am HIS child

Sweet Memories

When memories like a river flow
Take me back so many years
Those days I grew to love you so
We shared so much, both fun and tears

Remember love songs they were singing
We sang as you strummed your old guitar
That shiny new one in the driveway
Can't compare with your old battered car

Sweet memories steal into the twilight
Take me back once more to long ago
Softly hold me once again in the silence
With only echoes of sweet sounds
I used to know

Deserted City

This I know, this house is mine!
My taxes I have paid
I should have gone when others left
But, like a fool, I stayed

Here I am in this dull gloom
Suburbia left behind
Like migratory birds they fled
To gain their peace of mind

Though some return, now and then
I am never more to see
The bustling streets of yesteryear
This "city" used to be

Birth

A room full of love,
of awe and wonder of
the birth of a child

The nurses and doctors'
urgent encouragement
for the mother to push
when the time was right

Their constant help in every way
to make it a day to remember
The "Dad's" presence,
and also his strong yet gentle help

The relatives waiting,
silently praying all goes well
How could one express
the fervent joy the moment
a new life enters the room?

What a day of renewed
awareness of
The miracle of life!

Family

I went to see an uncle today
Who was sick and all alone
As I walked through the door
His face, oh how it shone!
He said I looked so pretty
Then explained it all this way
My presence there said so much,
Put some pleasure in his day

The face of a loved one
Is a joy to behold
It's not about their beauty
We connect to their soul
Love has no boundaries
Of distance or of time
It is strictly a heart thing
It's not ruled by the mind

Our connections with the family
Give us love and hope to share
It's in this safe surrounding
That children learn to care
From there we go into the world
To make some changes there
If each of us just touch one life
Save someone from despair

I Have

I have walked a lonely path in valleys
winding around the wooded hills
I have climbed the hills and looked down
upon valleys with rivers flowing
gently towards their destination
I have walked a railroad track in winter
when the wind blew cold and hard against
one poorly clothed against its frosty touch

I have spent lonely sleepless nights
waiting for the first faint light of dawn
To give promise of a new and brighter day
I have toiled long hours in the heat
of a southern sun and shivered
on many northern winter mornings

I have planted seed,
I have gathered the harvest
I have given birth and watched
our children grow into adulthood
I have read and studied to learn
what those before me had gained
I have never visited a foreign land
Some may say I am poor in material things
I feel rich in a spiritual sense, because
If I looked back on my life as a script for a play,
It could be a masterpiece!

Patriotic.....

The Veteran of Foreign War

He is older, his eyes are different now
They will never be the same
Not the smiling eyes of an innocent lad
Before the Selective Service filed his name
Shortly thereafter shipped to a foreign land
He is now a soldier, must daily face the enemy
Where bombs and guns cut short young lives
The awful price to keep a country free

How can the average person, never facing war,
And so far from home, know how it feels
When a comrade dies, or the fear of dying out
there alone
Let us never forget the lives that were lost,
Nor should we forget to say a prayer
For those who survived and one day returned
But left their innocence there

A memory of war changed forever
The way they think of our world
A tear to the eye, a rush of the heart
Each time our flag is unfurled

*This poem dedicated to my dear friend Granville
"Whitey" Helmick, served in the Army, 1st Cavalry
1949 – 1951, Korean War. I said goodbye to my
friend November , 2005, during the publication of this
book. He will be missed.

Americans Forever

It started as an ordinary day
But, Oh no!!
There were planes in the sky
Four would crash
Thousands would die
The thought to Americans
Would never begin
That we harboured people
Capable of so great a sin!
There was heroism
That day in the sky
Cell phones in hand
Telling loved ones goodbye
As brave firemen rushed
To site of first plane crash
Meeting others who escaped
Before that whole building collapsed
The sudden rude shock
The sheer disbelief
The mounting sadness
Anger, and such horrific grief
Not only the New York skyline
Was suddenly changed forever
Hopes and dreams of so many families
The focus of human endeavor
The aftermath of shock
Fearful feelings, nerves shattered
We were all reawakened
To what really mattered
The patriotism of Americans
Forever intact
Renewed resolve to
Be swift to react
With whatever it takes
To keep this great land "free'
Our Flag, may it always wave
Over America
For all the world to see!

A Mothers Prayer

Are there angels on the battlefield
To take our loved ones home?
This son of mine, so dear to me
Is a soldier far from home
I know he is in grave danger there
Please don't let him face it alone
Just let him feel your presence
I know you'll help the just to win
When peace shall come, battles won
Bring him home safe again

When the enemy wins, someone falls
Send messenger angels to "battle zones"
To let men know they died not in vain
As they take our brave soldiers home

Myriad Tragedy Never Ending

Super highway streaming with tin caskets
Coming from nowhere, going somewhere
Rushing as if a "grand prize' awaits them

Major explosions sending rockets into the blue
Planes forever crashing into the earth
With a noise louder than the screams,
however shrill

In every home a square of glass keeps
flashing faces
Voices speak endlessly, telling of these awful
events

Guns smoking where no war was declared
Wounded children bleed and die,
Fathers retaliate, Mothers cry

Drugs' Tragedy

Oh why? Why does one need to get high?
Isn't life itself enough to live
To work, to play, to love and give,
To reach, to stretch and grow
To help others to learn and know,
That friends and family, all those we meet
Even the stranger we pass on the street
Are all connected in this lowly sphere
Let us walk softly and lend and ear
To share whatever is troubling their mind
Is there a deeper need of someone to be
kind?

I'm weary of losing so many, so young
Those whose song will never be sung
Away with crack, and all other drugs
Streets alive with thieves and thugs
For their never ending need to get high
They need some money to buy a bigger
supply
Such a loss, so young saying goodbye
Because somewhere later, they lay down to
die

Faith

When our real self is tested
When trials come our way
When all we hoped or dreamed
Is rudely swept away
When our wretched heart is crying
Bereft of plan or plot
When those we love turn away
Our soul is all our lot

That is when faith sustains us
We cling so desperately
That is when we search our soul
For the key to set us free

Unlock the fear of failure
Look for a great new plan
The one who watches over us
Can inspire the hearts of man

So reach for the highest plain
Don't give up to defeat
Victory is just ahead of you
Each challenge you can meet!

The Motto

Procrastinate just long enough
To decide which path to take
Then I must proceed, oh yes indeed!
I must not hesitate!

For life is short, the days rush by
To delay is my undoing
Be swift to act, with wisdom and tact
Pursue what deserves pursuing!

A dream can become reality
If only we make a decision
To put to use, without excuse
The talents we've been given!

Loves...

Agnes Caldwell

Touching Me

If I were an artist
I'd paint your picture
Hang it for the whole world to see
But no brush on canvas
Could ever convey
The warmth when your hand touches me

That one time last winter
I had a bad fever
It had been a long night for me
I awoke next morning,
So glad it was over
Then I felt your hand touching me

When we're at a party
A stranger walks over
I wonder just where you can be
The band gets together
It's our song they're playing
Then I feel your hand touching me

Wherever I may travel
Whatever the conditions
I'll smile for the whole world to see
Just knowing you love me
Makes my life a pleasure
I know by your hand touching me

Unspoken Love

Love that has a thousand words
and cannot speak
is like barren sands on the desert,
lying lifeless on a desolate bed
until flames devour and
it becomes transparent like
sands burned into glass,
to be seen through as though
it didn't exist at all

Agnes Caldwell

I Vow to You My Love

*I give to you my love,
my hand, my heart
Just as my soul is in
God's keeping,
my body shall rest beside
you in peace,
Knowing your love, your devotion
is steadfast and sure
I, my love will share
always the delight of
Our togetherness
To share a moment with
you gives new meaning
to eternity
With fervor and commitment
I vow to you my love.*

Sunset Love

Slowly together, we walk hand in hand
No need for saying
What we both understand
We are facing the sunset
Slowly now, its getting low
How swift the colors change
Once red turns to golden glow

Soon darkness will be creeping
Hiding beauty in the night
Look up, my love, what splendor!
Oh! The stars, they shine so bright
Calmness now, so quiet and peaceful
Nothing now for us to fear
We are blessed, our love grows sweeter
These are truly the golden years

Lost

Lost in a strange forest
Not a familiar tree in view
The sun is hidden by an ominous
Cover of overhanging darkness
Oh, to touch a warm familiar hand
To guide me out into the vaguely
Remembered delights of yesteryear
Once laughter came easily,
Tears dried quickly in the warm breeze of
summer

Must this be my fate when love is no more?
And one awaits dark slumber?
Oh, where is that hope, that quickening heart
of longing?
Gone, and in it's place a void
Emptiness of immeasurable depth
Sending dreams asunder
Alas, tis' so when love is gone

Alzheimer's

I go to see her,
I must you understand.
Sometimes she is so disoriented,
I weep when I leave her.
Sometimes when the hurt is deeper
Than the well where tears are,
This deeper hurt takes into account
All the times she was there for me,
In my worst times,
Now, in her worst times
I am so helpless to do,
But to pray that peace will
Abide with her.
There are no tears to relieve
This ache in my heart
I have this picture of her in her youth.
Her neatness and the kind
And gentle person she was.
Her presence made our house a home.
She was and will forever be
So dear to me.
I can pray that sometimes,
Just for a little while,
She may remember too,
Those days of yore...

Family....

Her Name is "Angelica"

She has the blue eyes like her
Grandfather
He died before she was born
Her hair is silky, and doesn't
behave as she moves so rapidly
She moves it from her face
with an impatient little hand

She enjoys her toys, but
sometimes seems unaware of them,
so lost she is in the company
of some imaginary friend or animal

On "special" occasions when
she is all dressed up in the
ruffles and ribbons of
Grandmas' design,
she is so like a picture in a
classic storybook for children

In these short years of childhood
innocence she plays,
not guessing how much she is
adored by so many
This love for her is so unconditional,
She only has to be her very lovable "little self"
Our "Angel"

Cell Phone

His arm looks permanently crooked
With hand to his ear
It holds the cell phone

It stays there as he walks,
While he drives on the freeway,
As he walks through the grocery,

He talks to an unseen listener
One wonders if he sleeps with
The ever-present cell phone
Attached to his ear

Suddenly A Widow

Oh, the wretched mornings upon waking.
The nights when everyone in their homes,
with its routine of familiarity.
Not uncaring, but their life is the usual.
My situation is the unusual.
This empty feeling will find a healing.
It's the supreme test,
I wonder if I can make it.
Can I face the world with its everyday changes
and problems, without my soul mate, my constant friend,
and that assurance that I am loved and wanted?
My grandma lost her home from a fire
that destroyed all their belongings.
The family escaped and with help of friends
and neighbors, rebuilt.
Almost before they could recover, Grandpa died
from a heart attack.
Grandma started sewing on a foot powered
sewing machine and kept her three teenage daughters
before Social Security was even in existence.
Some of my happiest memories of childhood
are of times we visited her home.
Always happy to see us, sharing the flowers from her garden.
She was the most respected lady in the county.
We often found her in her swing on Sunday,
reading her Bible.

I will need all the strength of character,
as well as faith to carry on.
I know who I am and by the inheritance
of that ancestral endurance, I will face each day
knowing that God to whom my Grandma prayed,
will answer me as well, and I can rest in
HIS everlasting love.

Grandma   Horn

The glow of a setting sun touched the silver hair
of the woman standing tall, erect in the end
of the row boat.
In her hand she held a long paddle,
which she put into the water for a gentle stroke,
just enough
to keep the boat moving slowly toward it's
mooring.
As the sloped end touched upon the sand,
she laid the paddle on the bottom of the boat
and came forward with such graciousness
and stepped onto the sand to greet
her waiting admirers.
I, not yet accustomed to the river,
was in awe of my grandmother's ease at,
what to me, was a little scary.
Later, after we had carried pails of water
from the spring halfway up the mountains
rocky road, we helped prepare and enjoy a meal
of vegetables from Grandma's garden.
The evening was spent listening to
tales of the lives of other relatives,
how our cousins were working to stay together
as a family,
after the death of both parents.
The wind whispered in the willows that grew
along
the banks of the Kentucky River.

A Neighbor , A Friend

A good neighbor is someone you say hello to
When you see them in their yard,
Or at the mailbox,
Or putting out the trash.
Sometimes when neither of you are too busy,
You can stay and chat a while.
If you know they are ill, or just feeling lonely,
You can stay and let them reminise about old
times.
Whatever seems to give comfort and renewed
spirit.
If need requires, you take them to a doctor
Or hospital. If the need is reversed
They would do likewise for you.
You exchange ideas, but are never
condemning.
Just being supportive of each other
In this sometimes rapidly changing world,
If I have a wish for anyone, it would be
That they would have good neighbors.
I had a good neighbor.
His name was "Joe."

Soul Gifts

*Thank you Lord, for a wonderful Mother
And Grandmother
Their teaching still directs me
On this sometimes rocky road of life
Though they are gone,
Their words are as real to me today,
As when I was just a child.
To inherit such wisdom and truth
was greater than mere worldly riches.
Thank you Lord, for the soul gifts.*

My Father

He is not a saintly spirit
He is simply just a man
I think he tries with all his might
To do the best he can
When I was a child, he looked so tall
But as I grew I saw that he
Was just as human, and imperfect
As we all are apt to be
We make mistakes, just like he did
Then go on from day to day
Trying hard to correct our flaws
To find the better way

Now as I've grown, I still see him
As my idol standing tall
But now I think he sees me
As his equal, no longer small
Not just one day is "Fathers Day"
But ever day I live
I'll remember who I am
And due respect I'll give
To the man who helped a child to grow
Never making impossible demands
Yet giving me what I would need
To become a better man

His Son

There's the tree Dad once planted
You can see how big it's grown
In the yard flowers are blooming
From the many seeds he has sown

In my heart memories linger
Of the stories he would tell
Of his life before I knew him
Lessons that he learned so well

Not to boast, just to tell me
Men explore life as they go
If they hope to reap a harvest
Then some good seed they must sow

Well, I listened to the wisdom
To the lessons he had learned
Youth careening down a highway
For adventure he had yearned

Yes, the years would be a teacher
Then he passed it on to me
That same desire for adventure
To become the man he had longed to be

His Things

They are just things, you say
The things he left behind
But to me they are connected
To the life he had in mind
The fishing pole, the box of lures
Speak of what he liked to do
Everything he ever touched
Gives me a different view
A hat he wore, a pair of boots
His blue Ford truck
He loved to drive
His Cub Scout and weebloe gear
He wandered not aimlessly
While he was alive
He busied himself with what he loved
Yet always still found time
To spend with those he cared about
He gave them quality time
Now that he is gone to a better home
I treasure all those memories of his life
He seemed to feel he had lived it well,
In spite of all life's strife
No one else can have the picture
I can't pass this to another
It's just the feelings and thoughts of him
Of the one who was his Mother

"Grandma"

There's an old four-room house
That is slowly falling down
On a hill above the highway
That we used to take to town

In summertime Grandma's house
Was the greatest place to be
Flowers bloomin' in the yard
And that big old maple tree

A place where little children could play
Happy all day long
A phonograph for the older ones
To play some gospel songs

Grandma's rockin' chair forever
Will bring precious memories
Of songs with inspiration
That we heard upon her knee

Her sweetness and devotion
To the children close at hand
Her arms a gentle harness
Holding gently as she can

The heartfelt slow rendition
"Rock of Ages" made me cry
And "Jolly Old St. Nicholas"
Filled with laughter, made me sigh

She passes on the lyrics
Of songs from long ago
I'll keep those feelings always
No matter where I go

I had the greatest Grandma
A child could ever know
She taught us all the Bible
And watched our family grow

There's an old four-room house
That takes me back in time
Where sweet memories linger
Of that apron-clad Grandma of mine

I had the greatest Grandma
A child could ever know...
Written by Agnes and daughter Judy Ann, in March of 1997

"Vincent"

Today Heaven is brighter
With the light of his love
On this earth he'd grown weary
But there was joy up above
Our Dear Father so loving
Has welcomed him up there
While we trusted and waited
For Him to answer our prayer

We prayed for his healing
So right here he could stay
We got so much pleasure
Just watching him at play
In our human condition
Not knowing of God's plan
HIS holy wisdom is purer
It's far greater than mans

As the gates opened wide in welcome
A new angel gazed in awe at perfect day
Then his eye fell on a face so familiar
The hushed choir was touched to hear him say,

"Hello, Grandpa, lets write Mom a letter
We'll tell her not to cry anymore
Tell her to visit Grandma on Sunday
Someday they'll join us here, on Heaven's shore
Tell Daddy I love him so dearly
I know he'll be brave for Mommy, too
Tell him just to trust in Our Father
He'll send an angel there to tell him what to do."

So, please Heavenly Father
Hear a less selfish prayer
Just bless that new little angel
Give him happiness up there
Help our grief while we're missing
His sweet presence down here
Then reunite us in Heaven
Where you'll dry every tear

Grandma

Johnny

He must see life as a great adventure!
He always wears this happy smile
He gets right into this game of soccer
No cast on his legs in quite a while

His hair is a golden silken halo
Eye lashes long, dark, and curled
To show off that special sparkle
Constantly beaming at our world

Ever vigilant, tirelessly observing
Hoarding knowledge as he goes
Brilliant, obedient, and loving
Where life will take him, no one knows

He shows respect for his teachers
Granny and Papa's home is a special place
When Dad comes home in the evening
The garage becomes their private space

He enjoys Moms home cooked special dinners
The romp and play with his dog Spot
His sister Angel often reads him a story
It's easy to see Johnny enjoys life a lot!

Jeff

I remember a little boy
Who seemed mature beyond his years
He would meet a challenge with action
He had no time for tears
It seemed to me, that "life" to him
Was a journey to pursue
He always busied himself with plans,
Forever finding things to do.

His health, to others a great concern
Could never slow his pace
He just kept doing whatever he could,
Often with a smile on his face

Maybe he knew deep in his heart,
That life would be short, at best
Surly he lived, as if for him,
There was no time for rest

Sometimes I think God gives us
A loan to help us receive
His purest form of love and faith
We only need to believe

I remember a child who grew to become
A very brave young man
He gave life his best, could that courage and zest
Give us a glimpse of Gods' plan?

His life did not end in a violent way
Nor in a hospital wracked with pain
He went to sleep, then slipped away
Never to awaken on this plane

No need to linger, nor apologies to make
Life's work was completed now
He knew we would grieve and miss him
Yet we must go on somehow

Someday we know we'll meet him
In a land that knows no pain
What joy! when his face we see!
Yes Jeff, we'll be a family again!

Diana

She was much more than a Princess
That's what all the people say
Oh, such a tragedy
that she died that way

She was moved with such compassion
For those she saw in need
For one so blessed with material things
This gift seemed rare indeed

To reach out and touch the lowly
To show her gentle smile
Alas, that night on a Paris street
In such a little while
The world was stunned to hear the news
"Princess Diana did not survive"
The shock echoed around the world
To all who were alive,

Then grief began for all who cared
In days that were to come
For many days they came with flowers
And heavy hearts they carried
How many years ago they had watched
As she was married
So young, so innocent back then,
We watched her through the years
We knew she had trials of her own
And she shed some lonely tears

Yet she rose above her cares and strife
To heed a higher call
The world may have a better awareness
Of humanities
Since "their Princess" gave her all

83

Thoughts and Feelings...

Dear Children

You may say I'm beyond fifty
You can think I've had my day
But let me tell you children
Here is what I'd like to say

I'm still a human person
With hopes and dreams of life
You may think, "a hopeless widow"
Yes, I've been somebody's wife
I helped him raise our children
To pursue their own success
To meet and wed a partner
To share love and happiness

I still have some ability
A mind that still can plan
With health and hopes endurance
To live, I think I can

With your consideration
My dreams I will pursue
Please treat me with the same respect
I've always given you!

Aspiring

Tarry not amongst the thorns
But walk in Eden's flowers
Look not upon failures face
But look to higher powers

Walk not upon a wayward path
But walk on life's main highway
Your song may be a trumpet for
Some soul lost on a byway

A depressed soul can never be
A light to those who wander
Life's greatest talent is to share
My gift I will not squander

Yesterday my path was smooth
Today on rocks I stumble
Tho' I may dwell in palaces
Some need will keep me humble

Depression

*Sinking, sinking, spiraling downward
Nothing to grab onto, can't brake the fall
Hopeless, lost, desperate
From an insurmountable loneliness
Inadequate resourcefulness,
Lacking initiative,
Incapacitated as to any will to conquer
This indefinable darkness
An unutterable scream raging within
Unheard by an uncaring world*

Resolution

In the lingering purple twilight
Fear adorned in robes of gray
Anguished hours of total darkness
Cannot escape on feet of clay
Paralyzed into submission
Self descends into nothingness
Abandons all unique existence
Fear has won in totalness

But Oh! The rival here is courage
Of hope and faith she was born
Light and laughter are her virtues
Fadeth not neath eyes of scorn
Her delight is in the sunrise
To search for wisdom is her goal
Her riches are in understanding
At peace with body, mind and soul

Brides Bouquet

I watched her walking to you
I saw your loving face
No one could guess that
I longed to take her place
I sat sedately in the pew
By those who love you so
I hid my hurt behind a smile,
The others must never know

Then with tear-filled eyes
I heard you say your vows
Sealed them with the wedding kiss,
My dreams are over now

No one could guess that in the crowd
Of those who wished you well
Was one whose heart was breaking
I'm sure no one could tell
I kept my secret for so long
It had to be that way
I'm just the girl in the crowd
Who caught your brides' bouquet

Crazy

If I write it from the heart
It may sound crazy
But crazy is where I've gone
From missing you

I put the cat in the closet
Then opened the back door
I turned off the TV
Then watched it some more
I went to the window
To get me a drink
Looked out the sink
And started to think

Is this what happens
When they take you away?
Is this major depression?
Is it here to stay?
You see how it is
From missing you

Mirrored Confrontation

The face in my mirror I hardly know
Where did youth with its beauty go?
That face I remember with clarity
Unlike this stranger who stares back at me

The cheeks were firm and smooth as could be
The eyes were brighter and smiling with glee
That certain glow of youth at it's best
How little I knew then, of life's bitter test

This face has more shadow, less glow
Here and there deep lines are starting to show
This mirrored reflection of heartache and pain
Tight muscles gone slack from too much strain

Allows a little sag to appear here and there
With sinking heart I stand here and stare
Yes I stare at this stranger, is it really me?
What happened to the person I'd hoped to be?

The change must have happened quite gradually
I had just been too busy to stop and see
The subtle changes on through the years
Now I can't waste my time in melancholy tears

I must accept this face as a chapter I've read
And daily go forward to whatever is ahead
If, as they say, each life is a story to tell
I guess one could say, this face tells it quite well

A Creative Soul In Exile

I've known poverty Lord,
But when will it end?
I have walked the lonely railroad
Feeling I didn't have a friend
Lord, I've walked those railroad ties
With feet bare and calloused
Feet that didn't own a pair of shoes
I felt the splinters puncture,
Touch sensitive flesh
Then the highway where summer's hot sun
Brings tar to its surface
Bubbles burst on feet unprotected
I've worked the fields
Till my hands blistered, cracked and bled
I longed for escape.
When will the misery end?
Then the cleaning plant.
More work, more heat,
Suffocating steam that accidentally
Burns hands, arms that stay in motion
Endless motion, backbreaking drudgery
Lord, when will it end?
If you had a plan for me,
Please reveal it soon,
Please Lord, let it be soon!

Devotions...

Let Us Share

In your eyes I see a longing
A need yet unfulfilled
I hope you will let me share it
I wonder if you will

They say two hearts can master
What one cannot do alone
Am I reading it correctly?
What I think your eyes have shone.

Just let me be a partner
And help you to define
The thing you think is missing
To give you peace of mind

I know that love is healing
So if you are so inclined
Just remember I am waiting
For you to say you are mine

Written for Audrey and Karl, July 1998

Unspoken

Treat me gentle and I'll be strong enough to weather any storm, as long as I feel your love and devotion.

A loving gesture can break an ugly silence that screams with indifference.

A smile across a crowded room conveys the warmth of a thousand candles.

A soothing quietness, the very zenith of silence.

Please let us share the bright and pleasant side of the unspoken.

My Valentine

Somewhere in this busy world
We'll find a quiet place
Someday we can sit down
I'll look at your dear face

I'll tell you all that's in my heart
I know that you'll be kind
But I'm hoping you will say
You've known it all the time

I hope your heart is filled with love
The kind forever true
Not just a pretty valentine
I long to be with you

If my dreams should ever be
I'll spend my life with you
We'll share always what we hold dear
A love forever true

The Wedding

Two young lovers stand out
From the crowd
She so radiant
He so proud
Only moments ago
They said their vows
From this day forward
They will be together now

The faces of loved ones
Smiling and gay
Each with happy wishes
As they go away
A day filled with memories
To forever hold
Through a lifetime together
Through a story untold

Golden Ring

There are myriad song poems written
About many many things
Voices lifted high sing of love
And golden wedding rings
Somehow it never seems to touch
The way I really feel
This goes beyond poetic dreams
I know this love is real
I know I'll stand beside you
Walk that extra mile
When the party is over
I'll greet you with a smile
I'll be here in the morning
As the birds begin to sing
There is more to deep devotion
Than a golden wedding ring

Unfeathered

Like a bird
Who needs its freedom
wings spread
It takes flight
With swiftness
Of the wind
No time to consider
What may be right

Soar high!
My unfeathered friend
Soak up the sights
From far above
Watch for a sign
Somewhere aloft
You just flew
Away from "love"

Love's Glow

In the magic of the evening
When the lights are burning low
Now your arms are so inviting
Lost in loves romantic glow
Will we feel the same tomorrow?
In the noonday brilliant light
Will your arms still enfold me?
Just the way they do tonight

Is this love to last forever?
Will you seal it with a ring?
Are you filled with deep emotion?
Is tonight a passing fling?
These are things my heart is asking
Give it time and if it's right
We'll go on forever after
Just the way we are tonight

Loving Thoughts

Magic moments
Woven in mystery
Fleeing so fast
Fade into history
Mornings so sweet
Having you here with me
Enchanted evenings
Nights of ecstasy

Angels Whisper

Soft light gently touches your pillow
It's the dawn of an enchanted day
The joy of your warm love so precious
Helps the sunlight to brighten our way

You're the one to cheer me through sadness
Since we met I have felt just the same
I'll be there my dear if you need me
In my dreams angels whisper your name

When the clouds bring darkness or shadows
If it seems there's no good things in sight
I wait for your arms to embrace me
Then the warmth of your nearness at night

Each morning you're right here beside me
All day it's neither fortune nor fame
Just evenings to be with you, Darlin'
In nights dreams angels whisper your name

Love

Like an eagle in flight
Wings spread, soaring upward
Love enjoys its freedom
No one can bind or imprison it
To exist at all,
It must have its own way
At will the mighty eagle
Sweeps earthward gracefully
Loves pleasure may bring
A little sadness, hope deferred
Yet no other emotion
Gives so much to
Those who allow it to be
Soaring free!!

The Same Old Way

Are you really back to stay?
Would you hurt me once again?
We're too old for playing games
To be deceitful is a sin

Can I trust the words you say?
Seems I've heard them all before
Long ago the same old way
Till one day, you closed the door

Tell me now what can I plan?
Must I live from day to day?
Then deserted once again
On my own, the same old way

Tell me now, are you sincere?
Am I only potter's clay?
Later broken on the floor
To be rudely swept away

I -- C – U

As life hangs in the balance down the hall,
One waits for words of assurance.
Any sight of a doctor brings anxious eyes to
focus,
grasping for any hope of improvement.
Naked need of emotional comfort.
Need one wonder if love still exists?
Just sit in a waiting room of I C U
We live, we die,
Love lives eternal.

Prayers
and
Encouragement....

Agnes Caldwell

Rest

His body lies resting now
on a graceful hill,
surrounded by trees

I haven't been there at sunrise
but I know the birds sing in the treetops
and the breeze carries their
harmony heavenward

Are they singing the song
he was trying for so many years to perfect?
A song of love, security, and peace

May angel voices echo a sweet refrain
in the hearts of his children

Agnes Caldwell

Wings of Rapture

As I teeter precariously
On the cliff's edge,
Peering into fathomless gloom,
Terror rises
Screeching to be heard,
My eyes ache from gazing
Into frightful depths
Where unknown horrors await

But lo, behold!
A pair of wings
Clutching them to me
I sail swiftly away
Upward, ever higher
Far over the despair
That almost claimed me

Day of Hope

Oh, let this be the day of God's revealing
The power of love from peaceful hearts
To sinsick souls a healing
Bless this soul that I may be
A channel through which love can flow
Let wisdom guide my feelings

Agnes Caldwell

Weepin' Robin

A bird whose wing is broken
Won't even attempt to fly
A lover whose heart is broken
Will sit alone and cry

She is like a wounded robin
She must be alone to weep
The night seems filled with danger
She dares not restful sleep

Dreams filled with yesterday
When life held so much more
Now just empty nothingness
Can't guess what lies in store

But wait until the morning
Tomorrow's sun may rise
And dry the tears of yesterday
And mend the heart that cries

Storm Shelter

When the soul reaches out in terror despair
When debris of our belongings, our treasures,
fills the air
Our life hangs in the balance amidst the
loudest shrill
In poignant moments fearing,
Yet trusting in God's will

We trust in God's redemption
His mercy on our soul
While this mortal body shivers, in agony and
cold
Our spirit finds a mooring; it's anchored in
God's grace
We are safe whatever happens
HIS love is in this place

Angel Visit

The Lord sent an angel
To brighten our days
Just here for a visit
He really couldn't stay

How can we feel cheated?
When so richly we were blessed
God merely called Vincent home
Knowing how badly he needed rest

Now Heaven seems nearer
So many family members there
We need not be crying because,
We know someday, somewhere
We will surely be welcomed
In the crowd around the throne
When our Lord and our loved ones say,
"Come, welcome home!"

Atonement

Talents far greater than my own
Some other may possess
At times remiss to use what I have
Of this I must confess
For what I neglect I must atone
I can't blame it on another
That secret self known only to me
Not even to friend or brother
So let me give of what I have
The world may accept or refuse it
If naught it brings I'll simply say
"T'was a gift, I did not choose it."

Dear Lord

Dear Lord, here I am in the third phase of life.
I was so busy during the years, I had so many
lives depending on my help.
It must seem as if I put you on "hold" and
forgot.
I didn't forget. I'm sure you understand.
When so many voices are seeking attention we
are limited in this human condition.
I only hope I had learned enough to give the
right answers.
Now I am starting another phase, or is this just a
continuation of our spiritual unfolding, like a rose
until its beauty is spent, and it too dies.
Now as my body makes adjustments, so let my
mind and spirit make the necessary changes, to
accept life in all it's beauty and mystery.
Let me be patient with the young ones as they
struggle to find their way in this complicated
world.
Let me not be too quick to disagree with their
choices.
Let me consider them capable of right thinking.
Knowing that life itself teaches so much.
You made it so.
Thank you Lord for the "golden" years, too.

His Will

What is the greater purpose
For the life I live today
What high immortal law
Is mine to obey
As I struggle on and upward
I find I'm erring still
I ask in prayer each morning
To help me do His will

I find more joy in evening
Reflecting on my day
I have sweet peace of knowing
HE led me all the way

Lord, thank you for your caring
Your gentle guiding hand
The sun that warms our planet,
For trees that dot the land
Just bless the gentle breezes
And calm the mighty sea
Help us all to be humble,
May we trust Dear Lord , in Thee.

I Pray

Oh, God, please heal this hurting
Fill this empty void with joy
Make the past happy memories more vivid
So as to overshadow this most recent loss
Take away anxious feeling of responsibility
That do not belong to me

You give life, and You alone know each heart
You loan us a child for us to care for and
teach
You know this child will teach us more about
you
Our helplessness, our need to trust,
Our limitations, all the things that make us
humble in your presence
Please enlighten me as I stumble
through this uneven rocky valley
looking for the peace
only YOU can give

Hope

Out of the depth of hurt
A healing must start
Slowly a ray of light
Will dry tears in the heart

The nights darkest hour
Must recede into day
With dawn comes sunglow
Chasing shadows away

God gives us the power
To endure Satans' lure
A strength we can count on
Of faith kind and sure

Up and Onward

I'm standing in the doorway
Of something so divine
I see a splendid future
Just what I need is mine

I will not be discouraged
By those who doubt and whine
I'm resting in Gods promise
And in His will divine

I know if He is in it
There's sure to be success
I'm moving on with faith for
My life and happiness
I'm just a child He is leading
With humbleness, I pray
Help this meek soul
As I stumble on my way

The Master

What would the Master have me do?
As I travel this road of life
What could I say, or do?
That would ease another's strife
Could I carry part of a travelers load?
And therefore make it lighter
Could I by saying some kind words,
Make someone's day a little brighter?
Since I shall travel this road just once
I'd like my life to be
A reflection of God's gracious love
He freely gives to me
For as God gave through His only Son
Redemption for our sins
He gives His love to a thoughtless world
Through the acts of humble men

My Humble Prayer

If I should inherit great wealth some day
I wonder if I could still humbly pray
Or would I be like some people I know
Who so carelessly and proudly go?
With never a thought of the poor and needy
If I were wealthy would I be so greedy
Lord, fill my soul with grace and love
That I might always look above
For Thy gently and guiding hand
Wherever I travel in this, Thy land
For though, great things are built by man
The oceans are still at Thy command
The winds are at peace whenever YOU speak
In Jesus name, keep me humble and meek

My Passing

If it should be winter whenever I go
I hope my grave will be blessed
With a fresh blanket of new snow
Don't grieve for me whatever you do
I will ask our Lord to be always
Very near to watch over you

When you remember days we spent,
Looking back it's surprising how fast those
days went,
Just smile if you remember some funny thing
Memories may sometimes bring a touch of
sadness,
But don't tarry there, remember good times,
And find strength to share

If it should be spring, new life mocking death,
Fresh new leaves, blossoms and birds building
their nests
Singing their song, think of it as symphony of
celebration
Of my transition,
Then days since our parting will not seem so
long

Don't Grieve For Me

*My dear children will you listen
I just wish to let you know
The years have flown, this old body is weary
Someday soon I'll have to go*

*But let me leave you, not to grieving
Rather your heart be light with cheer
My life of love I lived it fully
Yes, I enjoyed my journey here*

*Yet another home beyond that mountain
The light so bright it beckons me
I know when I shall leave this homeland
A life of splendor is awaiting me*

*So live your life enjoy its pleasures
Some trials too, I know you'll see
Just rest secure in God's promise
Trust his grace and you will see*

*Someday away beyond that mountain
You will look beyond, and then I'll see
The faces I have loved so dearly
So my dearest ones
Don't grieve for me*

I can see them all
Their faces so sad
They wouldn't be so bereaved
If they knew the life I've had
Why, I could tell them of places
They just wouldn't believe!
Then they could smile
Instead, they sit and grieve

Now a spirit of light and love
In wonder unfolds before me
Visions of worlds I've yet to see
I don't long to go back
Here no worry, no heartache, I'm free
So please tell my friends
Please, don't grieve for me!

About The Author

Agnes Horn, born in the hills of Kentucky on December 27th, 1930, the fourth daughter, and fourth in line of eleven children born to Pryse and Hettie Horn.

She married Herbert Ray Caldwell in 1950, and together they moved to Detroit to make a life together. Early in their marriage, due to necessity, she began what became a 40-year career at Freydl's Clothing Store and Dry Cleaners in Northville, Michigan. It was here Agnes began writing, amongst rows of expertly cleaned and pressed clothes. On occasion a customer would request a poem or two.

Married forty-one years, they raised five children and had seven grandchildren, when in 1991, Ray succumbed to cancer. That same year, Agnes lost one of their beloved grandchildren, Vincent.

Through life's ups and downs, Agnes' writing ability seems to guide her through those experiences, both pleasantly and painfully. In her writings, you can clearly see the member of "International Society of Poets"

" *Sometimes it is with a mixture of emotions I look back at our life on Chapel Street. Forty-seven years may seem like a long time to someone. However, when we moved there I was a young mother of three. Later, two more daughters were added to our family. Needless to say, life was filled with a lot of activity. We had friendly neighbors and the children had friends to enjoy summer days and school days as well. We saw graduations and weddings.*

Grandchildren came. Some neighbors moved far away. Some, we still keep in touch. We attended many funerals. It's hard some times, to realize how many changes the last few years have brought.

I'm now alone fourteen years since my husband's death. Then a year ago, the shock of losing my only son Larry was hard to get through. I now have four daughters, ten grandchildren, five of whom are married, and four great-grand daughters. I'm still working full time. At age 75 I feel well and enjoy family get togethers. I have written when some of life's experiences overwhelmed me. If someone can get any comfort or enjoyment from this collection of poems, I'm rewarded."

Agnes